# CROSSING FLIGHT

*a Legion Cycle play*

*Erin Lerch*

I0139724

**BROADWAY PLAY PUBLISHING INC**
New York
www.broadwayplaypublishing.com
info@broadwayplaypublishing.com

First edition: May 2023
I S B N: 978-0-88145-985-2

Book design: Marie Donovan
Page make-up: Adobe InDesign
Typeface: Palatino

CROSSING FLIGHT received its world premiere production with TC Squared Theatre in January 2018. The cast and creative contributors were:

MEL ................................................... Lyndsay Allyn Cox
LAIONE ................................................... Blair Nodelman
SHEENA ...................................................Nicole Ventura
TROUT ...................................Alexander Joseph Muñoz
HAZE...........................................................Hayley Spivey

*Director*...................................Rosalind Thomas-Clark
*Assistant Director*.................................................Amy West
*Scenic design*...................................................Ben Lieberson
*Lighting design* ......................................Jeffrey E Salzburg
*Costume design*............................... Stephanie K Brownell
*Sound design*...........................................................Jay Mobley
*Stage Manager* ...........................................Kailey Bennett
*Props/Assistant Stage Managers*................. Julia Fioravanti
Jadira Figueroa
*Makeup (*LAIONE*)*...............................................Tori Moline

# AUTHOR'S NOTE

CROSSING FLIGHT takes place shortly into the future of the continental United States, shortly after an alien Legion arrives and devastates human civilization. While most survivors now live under the thumb of the Legion, here and there, a few small groups of humans continue to survive.

This play is one work within the Legion Cycle, which consists of multiple plays and audio dramas that all live in the same post-alien-apocalypse universe, but also each work as a standalone story. The Legion plays are intentional acts of rebellion within the American theatre. Where most sci-fi stories for the stage focus solely on the human characters, the Legion plays feature multiple alien species onstage at once. There are always numerous queer and trans actors in roles that are about more than just being queer or trans. Legion stories use the presence of nonhuman characters to investigate who has the privilege of being treated as a person, and who is seen as an outsider.

A few things to keep in mind that I and collaborators have discovered while working on plays and stories in the Legion world, to give you a starting place:

Keep in mind that this play is set in our world, in our future. The characters are as aware of science fiction stories as we are now, and they are aware that they're living through one of those stories.

Pace is incredibly important in this play. Every moment is precious. There should be no pauses where they are not noted, and if in the rehearsal room you find that it makes more sense to run through pauses that *are* noted, go right ahead. Earn the silences. Make sure they're pushing the action forward.

When designing aliens, while I've compared them loosely to Earth animals (birds and rats, here), remember that they are not from Earth, and you are not limited to palettes found on Earth animals. Go nuts.

# CHARACTERS & SETTING

MEL, *a former fighter pilot. Woman. She/her pronouns.*

LAIONE, *LAY-own-ee. A Scout with the alien Legion. Avian. They/them pronouns.*

SHEENA, *a former soldier. Woman. She/her pronouns.*

TROUT, *a scientist. Nonbinary. Ze/zer pronouns.*

HAZE, *A Tracker with the alien Legion. Ratlike. She/her pronouns.*

*There are also nine voices that are only heard on the radio. A breakdown of radio voices is included at the end of the text.*

*The Pacific Northwest, Kaniksu National Forest. The basement of an old ranger station.*

*Time: The not too distant future.*

# CASTING NOTE

Trans and nonbinary roles in this play must be played by trans/nonbinary actors. While I have not labeled aliens' genders as a general rule, aliens with pronouns other than she/her or he/him must be played by nonbinary actors as well. That said, actors need not necessarily use the exact same pronouns as the characters—I would encourage trans and nonbinary actors to read for any parts that they feel are appropriate. I also encourage those casting this play to think expansively about the characters who may initially read as cisgender. Unless a character is specified as cis, the role is open to anyone who feels their identity aligns with the character's.

While the characters have not been written with a specific race in mind, under no circumstances should this play have an all-white cast, nor should the only actors of color be playing nonhuman characters. As you are making casting decisions, I encourage you to consider the role of violence in this play. Consider if your casting choices are playing into harmful dynamics that already exist. Specifically, think carefully about who is pointing a gun at whom in this play.

# TEXT NOTES

a / indicates where the next line should interrupt the current line.

A line break in a character's text indicates a new thought.

# Scene 1

(*Lights up on a dilapidated basement-turned-workroom. It is enormously cluttered. Something drips occasionally in the background. High up on the back wall are two thin, dusty windows, through which we can see that it is dusk. The room is dominated by one large table, cluttered with machinery and assorted parts. The walls are papered with sketches, designs, and blueprints, some of which are so water-damaged as to be indecipherable. An old radio sits in the corner. Next to the radio is an unknown device, cobbled together from scrap.*)

(*Something drones in the distance. It grows louder, passes overhead, and fades away.*)

(*The sound of a door opening. Labored breathing.* MEL *backs into view. On her back is a bulky, blood-stained bundle. Dark feathers may poke out between folds of cloth. She is dragging a body. The body,* LAIONE, *is humanoid but clearly nonhuman. In place of feet,* LAIONE *has large birdlike talons. Their hands are tipped with claws. Crumpled beneath them is a single damaged wing. They are deeply unconscious.*)

(MEL *drags* LAIONE *to the far side of the room. She stands, sets her bundle on the table, and fiddles with the device next to the radio. She climbs into the boxes, digging into one near the wall. Pause. She climbs back out. She retrieves an overstuffed medical kit from one of the piles. She kneels next to* LAIONE *and opens the kit. Pauses. Turns* LAIONE *over and unbuckles their belt. A gun is clearly visible hanging from the belt. She tosses it well out of reach. She begins to tend to a wound on* LAIONE's *leg.)*

*(Suddenly,* LAIONE *lurches upright, grabbing* MEL *around the throat.)*

LAIONE: What did you do?

*(*MEL *digs her knuckle into the leg wound until* LAIONE *releases her.)*

LAIONE: What happened? Where am I?

MEL: Whaddya say, Wings? Gonna let me finish patching you up?

LAIONE: Don't touch me, human.

MEL: Fine. Bleed out on my floor. No skin off my bones.

LAIONE: Who are you? What happened?

MEL: What do you remember?

LAIONE: I was patrolling. Over the mountain, heading towards the lake, like always. I thought maybe I saw something moving on the ridge, so I circled back. Then…I fell. No. I was shot down.
You shot me down.

MEL: No.

LAIONE: You're lying.

MEL: Why would I bother?

LAIONE: Because humans lie.

MEL: If I'd shot you down, why would I be helping you?

LAIONE: I don't need your help.

MEL: Hate to break it to you, Wings, but you kinda do.

LAIONE: My name is Laione.

MEL: Okay.

LAIONE: You keep calling me Wings.

MEL: Yeah?

LAIONE: Plural. *(Pause)* Did you cut it off?

MEL: No. I found it first. Then I followed the blood and broken branches and found you.

LAIONE: Where is my belt?

MEL: Why? You want to shoot me?

LAIONE: No. There's medspray.

MEL: Aha. *(She moves to get the belt.)*

LAIONE: Why are you doing this?

MEL: Patience. We'll get to that.

*(MEL brings the belt, sans gun, to LAIONE. LAIONE snatches it away.)*

MEL: You're welcome.

*(LAIONE pulls a small spray canister from the belt. They spray the leg wound. It closes.)*

MEL: It's gone.

LAIONE: It's standard issue.

MEL: We used to call it miracle spray. Never thought I'd see it up close.

*(MEL reaches for the can. LAIONE pulls it back.)*

MEL: What? Don't want to share?

LAIONE: Humans aren't—

MEL: Allowed? Hate to break it to you, Dorothy, but you aren't in Kansas anymore.

LAIONE: What?

MEL: You can't reach your back on your own.

LAIONE: As if I'd let you touch it.

MEL: You're gonna have to.
Tell you what. You let me help, I'll tell you why I'm
doing it. Deal?

LAIONE: …Deal.

*(They reluctantly hold out the can.)*

MEL: Thank you.

*(MEL examines LAIONE's back. It's a mess. She brushes
some dirt away and sprays.)*

LAIONE: You didn't tell me your name.

MEL: Didn't think you'd care. It's Mel. *(She sprays
again.)* This stuff is crazy. Is it good enough to reattach
your wing?

LAIONE: No. Even if it hadn't been…how long?

MEL: Most of an afternoon.

LAIONE: If I'd been in orbit, maybe. But it's too late
now.

MEL: Sorry. What would they do in orbit?

LAIONE: They have med baths.

MEL: Med baths?

LAIONE: I don't know how they work. That's Medic
knowledge.

*(MEL moves to touch their wing.)*

LAIONE: Don't.

MEL: We can do this all day, Wings. Unless you want
to lose this one, too.

LAIONE: No.

MEL: Then let me look at it.

LAIONE: Why? You're human. You wouldn't know the
first thing about how to fix it.

MEL: I wouldn't, except I used to keep birds, when I was younger. I figure the principle's the same.
Your call.

LAIONE: Careful.

MEL: This is a mess, but it doesn't feel broken.

LAIONE: It needs a med bath.

MEL: Don't have one. Humans aren't allowed, remember? We have to make do with stitches and side effects.

LAIONE: "Stitches?"

MEL: Sew it up, leave it to heal on its own. Takes weeks.

LAIONE: And you won't let me go to the Legion.

MEL: Would they help you?
I served in the war. I saw what they did when they cleared a battlefield. Didn't see any one-winged Scouts being carted back to camp.

*(The drone begins.)*

MEL: They'd kill you.

LAIONE: Maybe. Maybe it would be best.

MEL: Bullshit.

LAIONE: It'd be a mercy. Grounding is a slow death.

MEL: Who says you're grounded?

*(The drone is overhead.)*

LAIONE: What do you--?

MEL: Shh.

*(MEL listens, looking up towards the windows. The drone passes and fades into the distance.)*

MEL: You've got broken feathers. We need to pull those out so the new ones can start growing.

LAIONE: You've done this before?

MEL: Yes. Not on this scale, but.

LAIONE: Fine.

(MEL *finds a set of pliers. She spreads* LAIONE's *wing.*)

MEL: Brace yourself.

LAIONE: Do it already.

(MEL *pulls a feather.* LAIONE *grabs* MEL's *wrist.*)

MEL: Gotta be done, Wings.

LAIONE: Just…give me a minute.

(*After a moment,* LAIONE *releases* MEL's *arm. There's blood.*)

MEL: (*Matter-of-fact*) Ow. (*She sprays the wounds. She scrubs her arm clean on her pants; the wounds are gone.*) Huh.

(MEL *pulls another feather. She continues the process throughout the next section.*)

LAIONE: Why are you helping me?

MEL: Because I want something from you.
Did you think I'd say "out of the goodness of my heart"? I can lie to you if you want.

LAIONE: No.

MEL: Good news is, I think we can help each other.

LAIONE: Why would I help you? You're human.

MEL: And you're Legion.

LAIONE: I thought humans hated my kind.

MEL: We do.

LAIONE: But you're different?

MEL: Hardly.

LAIONE: Then what do you want from me?

(MEL *yanks the last feather.*)

MEL: To fly.

LAIONE: To *what*?

MEL: I want wings.

LAIONE: You're human. You can't have wings. And I'm grounded.

MEL: What if I could give you back the sky?

LAIONE: Don't taunt me.

MEL: I'm not. *(She indicates a drawing on the wall.)* Look.

LAIONE: That doesn't mean anything to me.

MEL: Look at the sketch. Biomechanical wings.

LAIONE: Impossible.

MEL: They said the same thing about my leg. *(She knocks on one thigh. It makes a metallic sound.)* Proved 'em wrong once.

LAIONE: If it were possible, the Legion would have done it by now.

MEL: Why would they? They had you. *(Pause)* I've tried before, but the musculature in birds is all wrong, doesn't translate to the human form, but you could be it. Even just from patching you up I've got a better idea of what I need. Give me a few days, maybe a week—

LAIONE: In return for my life, you expect me to help you fly? I'm Legion.

MEL: You're not listening. Help me do this, and I'll give you back your wings.

LAIONE: You're lying.

MEL: What if I'm not?

LAIONE: Then you're crazy.

MEL: Maybe. You see a better option?

*(A knock.)*

SHEENA: Mel? You in there?

MEL: Up. Quickly – she'll kill you if she sees you.

SHEENA: Mel?

MEL: Kinda in the middle of something.

SHEENA: Can I come in?

MEL: Just hang on, I'll come to you.

*(With* MEL's *help,* LAIONE *staggers to a closet on one side of the room.)*

MEL: Stay in there, no matter what you hear.

LAIONE: But—

MEL: Just do it!

LAIONE: Fine.

*(*LAIONE *half-collapses into the closet and* MEL *shuts the door. She takes a second to hide the evidence. There's too much blood to cover up. She answers the door.)*

SHEENA: Jesus, Mel.

MEL: It's not mine.

SHEENA: What happened?

MEL: You don't want to know.

SHEENA: I'll take your word for it.
What'd you do, slaughter a deer in here?

MEL: Like I said—

SHEENA: I don't want to know. You sure you're okay?

MEL: Positive.

SHEENA: What's this?

MEL: Wing from a Legion soldier.

SHEENA: You found it?

MEL: Clearly.

SHEENA: No, I mean, the birdbrain it was attached to. Did you find it?

MEL: Oh. No. Just the wing.

SHEENA: Where?

MEL: Why?

SHEENA: Shot one of the fuckers down over the ridge earlier. Was hoping I could get some good loot off the corpse.

MEL: You shot down one of the Legion. Sheena.

SHEENA: I know, I know, stupid risks. In my defense, the thing was circling back towards us. Maybe it saw something, I don't know. I didn't want to risk it. And it was a *beautiful* shot. Lined it up and—wham—right through the base of its wing. It looked like it went down on the south side of Pend Oreille, but when I went looking I couldn't find it. I didn't think even one of them could survive a fall like that, but… I wanted to come check, make sure you were okay, in case that thing is roaming around out there looking for revenge.

MEL: I'm fine.

SHEENA: I see that. Where'd you find the wing? Maybe I can get back there, track it down.

MEL: Let's see. *(She crosses to a map on the wall depicting the area.)* Somewhere around here? *(She points to a spot near the southern ridgeline.)*

SHEENA: Really? That far south? I could've sworn it was closer to the mountain.

MEL: Could be remembering it wrong.

SHEENA: Okay. I'll check it out, see what I can find. That's a long way to carry it back. What d'you need the wing for, anyway?

MEL: A project.

*(The drone begins in the distance.)*

SHEENA: That crap again? Mel, honestly.

MEL: What else have I got to do?

SHEENA: You could always—

MEL: I'm not helping the Rebellion, Sheena.

SHEENA: They could use you.

MEL: No.

SHEENA: Speaking of the Rebellion, did you hear? Badger, out east? She and her crew hijacked a Legion ship. They snuck into the compound at Omaha and flew it right out. Like, they actually got away with it.

MEL: I heard. She's gonna get herself and her whole team killed.

*(The drone is overhead. Both* MEL *and* SHEENA *wait for it to pass. It does, eventually.)*

SHEENA: At least she's trying.

MEL: Sheena.

SHEENA: Fine. You made a hell of a mess.

MEL: I'll deal with it.

SHEENA: Suit yourself. You got enough food?

MEL: Yeah.

SHEENA: Hunt tomorrow?

MEL: Sure.

SHEENA: Just…be careful out there. Those Scouts are tricky bastards.

MEL: You, too.

*(*SHEENA *exits.* MEL *waits a moment, then crosses to the closet and opens it.)*

LAIONE: She did it. She did this to me.

MEL: Calm down.

LAIONE: I'll tear her throat out. I'll rip her legs off, see how she likes being *maimed*, I'll— *(They stagger and catches themself on the table.)*

MEL: You done?

LAIONE: I'll kill her.

MEL: You'll have to go through me, first.

LAIONE: You think that would stop me?

MEL: I think a bullet in your head would. Though I'd rather it not come to that.
If it's any consolation, she meant to kill you.

LAIONE: This is her fault.

MEL: We didn't start this war, Wings.

LAIONE: You lost it years ago.

MEL: Some of us never accepted that.

LAIONE: You.

MEL: Me. Sheena. Others. Each in our own way.

LAIONE: Why?

MEL: Plain old human stubbornness, I guess.

LAIONE: You have to know it's pointless.

MEL: This was our planet, Wings.

LAIONE: Your planet. You were *ruining* your planet. Or have you forgotten already?

MEL: I remember.

LAIONE: You may not have started this war, but you started plenty of your own. Against each other. Against your world. How could we stand by and let that happen?

MEL: Is that the party line?

LAIONE: It's the truth. We brought you peace.

MEL: Funny how you had to bomb half the country into cinders to get there. God only knows what you did to the rest of the world, since you cut us off.

LAIONE: Not all of you fought. Some didn't.

MEL: What happened to them?

LAIONE: We left them alone. Mostly.

MEL: Mostly. Suppose it's better than what you did to us.

LAIONE: If you hadn't fought, we wouldn't have had to.

MEL: My parents had a farm in Oregon. Never fought a day in their lives. The Legion killed them, and every single animal on that farm.

LAIONE: They must have resisted.

MEL: Uh-huh. The cows put up such a fight that the Legion had to kill them.
Whatever helps you sleep at night. (A moment) I need a decision, Wings.

LAIONE: Do I really have a choice?

MEL: Sure.

LAIONE: Turn traitor or die, right?

MEL: Never said you had a good choice.

LAIONE: And you? You'd make a deal with the Legion? Doesn't that make you a traitor, too?

MEL: I'm not making a deal with the Legion. I'm making one with you.

LAIONE: Same thing.

MEL: Is it?

LAIONE: How do I know you won't just kill me when you have what you want?

MEL: You don't. How do I know you won't go tell the Legion on me as soon as you have what you want?

*(Pause)*

LAIONE: Why?

MEL: Why what?

LAIONE: Why do you want to fly?

MEL: Why do you care?

LAIONE: If you endanger the Legion—

MEL: I have no interest in fighting them. I promise you that.

LAIONE: If you can give me back—

MEL: I can.

LAIONE: What do you need me to do?

*(Transition. Full dark outside.)*

*(The following monologues occur over the action described in the stage directions. Fizzy, staticky radio broadcasts. Feel free to play with the order and the construction; maybe the radio fades back and forth, maybe not. The broadcasts do not need to line up with any particular stage direction.)*

RADIO 1:
At 0300 hours last night, Badger and a small team infiltrated the Legion compound in Omaha. At approximately 0415, they escaped with one of those Legion survey ships. The last we saw of them, they were heading north over Lake Huron with several Legion squadrons in pursuit. No further news at this time. We'll keep our eyes and ears open, as we always do.

*(MEL helps LAIONE to a cot in the corner. They lie down and fall asleep.)*

*(MEL finds a clean piece of paper and spreads it out on the table, sketches. Hangs the sketch on the wall: rough anatomy sketches of LAIONE's body and wing. The drone passes over. MEL ignores it.)*

RADIO 2:
This is Raven, reporting from the Norman settlement. They've been letting people send letters for a while now. Some people say they've heard back from family members in other places, who got trapped there when…when everything went down. They—the Legion – they're saying that they're going to start letting people travel between the settlements. Not sure how they're going to decide who to let go, but… Not sure I believe them at all, honestly. It seems too good to be true.

RADIO 3:
Nevada Web here. We're seeing some weird activity inside the Olympia Legion compound. We're not sure what's causing it yet, but if you're in the Northwest, keep your heads down and your eyes on the skies.

RADIO 4:
I'd like to pick up where we left off in Book One.

(MEL *unwraps the bundle and examines the bloody remains of* LAIONE's *wing. It's unsalvageable. She fiddles with the device next to the radio, then takes the wing outside, leaving* LAIONE *alone onstage.*)

(LAIONE *wakes. Gets up. Eyes the door. Instead, limps over to reclaim their belt and finds their gun amidst the debris.*)

(LAIONE *checks the gun is loaded. They go back to the bed and lie down, tucking the weapon out of sight.*)

"So Athena vowed and
under her feet she
fastened the supple
sandals, ever-glowing
gold, that wing her over
the waves and boundless
earth with the rush of
gusting winds. She seized
the rugged spear tipped
with a bronze point—
weighted, heavy, the
massive shaft she wields
to break the lines of
heroes the mighty
Father's daughter storms
against. And down she
swept from Olympus'
craggy peaks and lit on
Ithaca, standing tall at
Odysseus' gates, the
threshold of his court.
Gripping her bronze spear,
she looked for all the
world like a stranger now."

## Scene 2

*(The next day.* LAIONE, *asleep.)*

*(*MEL *enters, a bucket tucked under one arm.* TROUT *follows
her, humming jauntily.)*

*(*MEL *fiddles with the device next to the radio, then starts
removing newly-bleached bones from the bucket and laying
them out on the table.)*

MEL: Anything to eat? I've got rabbit jerky, deer jerky,
or cinnamon sugar PopTarts.

TROUT: PopTarts? Really?

MEL: Found some in my stash.

TROUT: You sure they're still good?

MEL: Pretty sure PopTarts are gonna outlast us all. Them and the roaches.

TROUT: I'm fine. Love what you've done with the place.

MEL: Worse last night. Looked like a slaughterhouse.

TROUT: Courtesy of your new friend here, eh?

MEL: Mm.

TROUT: Looks like about ten miles of bad road.

MEL: You should've seen them yesterday.

TROUT: Deep sleeper.

MEL: They demolished my stock of pain pills last night. Apparently, their field kits don't include anything for pain.

TROUT: Seems an oversight.

MEL: The Legion doesn't waste painkillers on cannon fodder.

TROUT: Don't tell me you feel sorry for them.

*(The drone in the distance.)*

MEL: God, no. Just don't see the point in pretending things aren't the way they are.

TROUT: Mm. Sheena know you saved this one?

MEL: No.

TROUT: You going to tell her?

MEL: Probably.

TROUT: Think you can hide it?

MEL: Probably not.

*(The drone is overhead.* MEL *looks up. It fades into the distance.)*

MEL: Is it just me, or was that closer than usual?

TROUT: No time to waste.

MEL: I figured it might be best to start with the bird. More to build on.

TROUT: Speaking of. You realize you don't have the musculature for wings, right? Biomech can only do so much.

MEL: Let me worry about that.

TROUT: Something I should know?

MEL: Ask me later.

TROUT: Think I can wake them up?

MEL: Better let me. They can be pretty quick with those claws.

TROUT: By all means.

*(*MEL *grabs a bottle of water and a packet of jerky. She squirts* LAIONE, *or throws the jerky at them, waking them.)*

LAIONE: What was that for?

MEL: Safer than shaking you. Here.

LAIONE: What's this?

MEL: Figured you might be hungry. You slept for a while.

LAIONE: Oh.

*(*MEL *goes back to work.* LAIONE *notices* TROUT.*)*

LAIONE: Who're you?

TROUT: A scientist.

LAIONE: What kind?

TROUT: A geneticist. You can call me Trout.

LAIONE: Isn't that a fish?

TROUT: Mhm.

*(A moment)*

LAIONE: You're here to help with the wings?

TROUT: I am.

LAIONE: What do you need?

TROUT: A look at your wing.

LAIONE: Be careful with it, human.

TROUT: I understand completely.

*(Ze shows LAIONE zer hand; severely burnt sometime in the past, covered in scar tissue, barely moveable.)*

TROUT: Happened right after you lot hit Earth. Docs said it'd be better to chop it off, go for a prosthetic. I said I'd rather keep it, and here I am.

MEL: Got yourself discharged.

TROUT: That was half the point. I know a losing battle when I see one. *(A moment)* My hand, your wing, Mel's leg. Maybe we should lop something off of Sheena, make it square.

LAIONE: With pleasure.

*(TROUT laughs.)*

LAIONE: If it had been on the battlefield…but it wasn't. It was a cheap shot.

TROUT: Cheap shots are the only ones we can get these days.
Well. Let's take a look.

*(Ze leans LAIONE forward and examines their back and wing. MEL continues sorting bones.)*

TROUT: Does it still hurt?

LAIONE: No.

*(The drone begins.)*

TROUT: We humans, when we lose a limb, sometimes we get phantom pain in that limb, like it still existed. Just one of those funny things about the human mind, I suppose. You ever hear of anything like that happening to a Legion soldier?

LAIONE: I wouldn't know.

MEL: People with injuries that bad are usually killed as part of the cleanup. Right?

*(Pause. The drone passes overhead and into the distance.)*

LAIONE: Yes.

TROUT: You can sit back. I'm done.

*(TROUT wanders over to look at the new sketch on the wall. A moment. LAIONE considers the food. Opens it and takes a bite.)*

LAIONE: What is this?

MEL: Jerky. Dried meat.
Don't like it? I have PopTarts if you'd prefer.

LAIONE: It's fine. It's good.

*(LAIONE notices what MEL is doing.)*

LAIONE: Those are my bones.

MEL: Yep.

LAIONE: You— That's—

MEL: Problem, Wings?

LAIONE: It's not right.

MEL: You weren't using them anymore.

LAIONE: That's—it's not right—

MEL: Didn't take you for the squeamish type.

LAIONE: I'm not squeamish, it's—it's sacrilege. Our remains are meant to be burned, not—

MEL: Do you want your wing back or not?

TROUT: Why burned?

LAIONE: It's—it's your essence being returned to the sky. In the smoke.

MEL: Your "essence" is still inside you, isn't it? You're still alive.

LAIONE: I guess.

TROUT: I'm sure Mel wouldn't mind burning them after she's done?

MEL: Sure.

TROUT: Okay?

LAIONE: Fine.

MEL: Don't watch if it bothers you.

LAIONE: It's fine.

*(A pause)*

MEL: What?

LAIONE: I thought there'd be more.

TROUT: You didn't know?

LAIONE: That's Medic knowledge. I've never had any reason to know.

MEL: The only reason there are this many is because at least one shattered in the fall. See? *(She finishes laying out the bones.)* Trout, mind bringing that over here?

*(TROUT carefully pulls the drawing off the wall and brings it to the table.)*

MEL: Four main bones.

LAIONE: That's all?

MEL: Looks like.

TROUT: Nature favors simplicity.

*(A knock at the door)*

MEL: That's Sheena. Trout, you got anywhere to be?

TROUT: Hold on, let me check my calendar.

MEL: Mind keeping Wings here company?

TROUT: I think I could fit that in.

MEL: Thanks. *(She goes to fiddle with the device.)*

LAIONE: What is that?

TROUT: You haven't told them?

MEL: I'm not a fan of threats.

LAIONE: Told me what?

MEL: This is…a contingency.
It's a bomb.

LAIONE: You're lying.

MEL: Kinda wish I was, honestly.

LAIONE: If it is a bomb, why would you tell me?

MEL: I figure lying to you would hurt the whole 'let's work together' thing. Besides, it's not for you. It's for the Legion. If they ever find this place.

LAIONE: Then why are you setting it now?

MEL: It's on a timer. If I don't come back in a few hours and deactivate it, kablooey. More reliable than a detonator.

*(A more insistent knock)*

SHEENA: *(Through the door.)* Today, Mel.

MEL: I'll be back tonight. *(She exits.)*

LAIONE: I thought I wasn't a prisoner.

TROUT: You want to leave, I won't stop you.

LAIONE: There's a *bomb*.

TROUT: It's perfectly safe. Mel knows I'd be thoroughly annoyed with her if she blew me up.

LAIONE: Right.

TROUT: You don't believe me?

LAIONE: I'm skeptical.

TROUT: Go ahead, then. Leave. *(A moment)* So. Tell me about yourself.

LAIONE: What do you mean?

TROUT: I thought it was a pretty simple question. Tell me about yourself. Your home planet. How you joined the Legion. Anything, really.

LAIONE: Why?

TROUT: Curiosity.

LAIONE: Don't you humans have a saying about that?

TROUT: I've never let it stop me.

LAIONE: My origin planet is near the galactic core, I'm told.

TROUT: You've never been?

LAIONE: No. My species colonized a few surrounding systems before we were assimilated. I grew up on one of those worlds.

TROUT: Assimilated.

LAIONE: The Legion absorbs whatever new species it comes across.

TROUT: All of them?

LAIONE: Yes.

TROUT: Not us.

LAIONE: We tried. You refused.

TROUT: Can you really blame us? You show up in orbit and demand we submit without so much as a 'hi, how you doing?'

LAIONE: It was for your own good.

TROUT: Aha.

LAIONE: It was. You were destroying each other and this planet. This is what the Legion <u>does</u>. It saves species from themselves.

TROUT: By killing us.

LAIONE: Some of you, yes. Because you just wouldn't give up. I believe the report said: 'suicidally stubborn, with an inherent drive to rebel."

TROUT: I think our bullheadedness is something to be proud of. It's certainly gotten us into enough messes as a species.

LAIONE: Doesn't that mean you should be trying to fix it?

TROUT: Too late now, isn't it?

LAIONE: I guess.

TROUT: So, what was your planet like? The one you grew up on.

LAIONE: Hot. It orbited a binary star system, two dwarves. More land, fewer oceans than here. The trees were huge. Big enough to sleep on a branch with no fear of falling. Everything was so much bigger there.

TROUT: Sounds a little bit like the redwoods.

LAIONE: Redwoods?

TROUT: Haven't you seen them? They're just west of here, near the coast. They're massive.

LAIONE: I've only patrolled this area. West is another flock.

TROUT: That's a shame. What color was your sky?

LAIONE: It was purple.

TROUT: Fascinating.

LAIONE: It doesn't matter.

TROUT: Why not?

*(The drone begins.)*

LAIONE: I can't go back.

TROUT: The Legion wouldn't let you?

LAIONE: That's not why.

TROUT: Why, then?

LAIONE: The same reason I can survive on this godsforsaken planet.

TROUT: They genetically modify scouts?

LAIONE: Yes. The atmosphere here is too thin for us, otherwise. We'd suffocate.

TROUT: Did they give you a choice?

LAIONE: No.

TROUT: Seems cruel.

LAIONE: I'm just a Scout. One of many.

TROUT: I'll admit I've done some shady things, but never without consent.

*(Pause. The drone passes.)*

TROUT: How does it work for assimilated species?

LAIONE: They determine what role your species is best suited for. Scout, Tracker, Medic, Overseer, whichever. Then they test children for military ability. If you pass, you join the army.

TROUT: For how long?

LAIONE: Until you earn the right to resign.

TROUT: How?

LAIONE: What do you mean?

TROUT: There must be rules.

LAIONE: Of course. Loyalty. Obedience. Strength.

TROUT: That's it?

LAIONE: That's all. Everything comes from that.

TROUT: So, say you're just the best Scout that's ever
been. You distinguish yourself in some big, exciting
way. Any chance you could become the Commander,
one day?

LAIONE: No.

TROUT: No?

LAIONE: I could become a flock leader, maybe. But the
Grand Commander is only ever Command.

TROUT: That doesn't seem fair.

LAIONE: What is your species' fascination with "fair"?
It works. That's what matters.

TROUT: What happens if you fail?

LAIONE: I won't fail.

TROUT: Sure, okay, you won't. What if a hypothetical
someone fails? What happens to them?

LAIONE: It depends which part of the Code they've
broken. If someone is weak, they're sent for retraining.
If someone is disobedient, they may be retrained or
imprisoned. If someone is disloyal...

TROUT: They're killed.

LAIONE: As they should be.

TROUT: Do you really believe that?

LAIONE: I believe the Legion's managed to keep eleven disparate species in line for centuries. Maybe millennia. It works.

TROUT: If you say so.

LAIONE: What about you? You don't seem military.

TROUT: I wasn't. Not really. I was recruited for a specific project.

LAIONE: What project?

TROUT: It doesn't matter. We didn't finish.

*(A moment)*

LAIONE: How long has Mel wanted to fly?

TROUT: As long as I've known her. We met during the war.

LAIONE: Why does she want wings? What purpose does it serve?

TROUT: You're asking the wrong person.

LAIONE: I asked her. Last night and again this morning. She won't answer. She dodges the question.

TROUT: Mel prefers to keep her personal life personal.

LAIONE: So she won't tell me.

TROUT: I can't help you there.

LAIONE: Do you think she means to keep her promise?

TROUT: Yes.

LAIONE: Even though I'm Legion.

TROUT: Are you? *(Pause)* Mel keeps her word.

LAIONE: I hope she does.

*(Transition. The windows darken to night. A drone approaches, passes by, and fades. The radio:)*

| RADIO 5: | *(MEL returns with food.* |
|---|---|
| This is Axolotl, in | *Checks and disarms the* |

Scranton. I know I've been quiet lately. I didn't want to do anything that might arouse suspicion. I've been trying to convince the Overseers to let us go back to New York. Spun them a story about important cultural artifacts in the ruins that we want to reclaim, something about boosting morale, yadda yadda. We're scheduled to go tomorrow. But it's been weird here, lately. Tense. Something's got them worried. They haven't said anything about canceling the trip, but… I wanted to check in, so that if I don't come back, someone will remember.

RADIO 4:
Tell me about yourself now, clearly, point by point. Who are you? Where are you from? Your city? Your parents? What sort of vessel brought you? Why did the sailors land you here in Ithaca? Who did they say they are? I hardly think you came this way

*bomb.)*

*(MEL sketches. TROUT works. LAIONE waches.)*

*(MEL gathers the bones. Jerks her head at LAIONE. They exit. A red glow becomes visible in one of the windows. The sound of fire crackling.)*

*(Alone onstage, TROUT searches the room. Ze finds LAIONE's gun. After a moment, ze replaces it and continues searching.)*

on foot! And tell me this for a fact—I need to know— is this your first time here? Or are you a friend of father's, a guest from the old days? Once, crowds of other men would come to our house on visits—visitor that he was, when he walked among the living.

RADIO 6

Croc, here. We hit a Legion supply depot today just outside of Meridian. Didn't want those fuckers to forget we're here while they're all so focused on Badger's little stunt in Omaha. They never saw us coming. We got food, medicine, some tech that we'll pass off to Aurora to see if they can take it apart. No casualties. All Ember factions, I urge you: remind them we're here. Remind them that they may have control, but they have not won until the last of us is six feet under. Remind them that we haven't given up. And if you see Badger, tell her I owe her a beer.

# Scene 3

*(A few days later. On the table are the beginnings of the wings.* TROUT *sits at one end of the table, tinkering with a biomechanical port the size of a CD.* MEL *works at the middle of the table.* LAIONE *watches.)*

MEL: Quit hovering.

LAIONE: What else is there to do?

TROUT: Come over here and let me see your back.

*(*LAIONE *does.)*

TROUT: Relax. I'm just checking something. This isn't the hurty part.

LAIONE: I'm not afraid of pain.

TROUT: Never said you were. Still, it's common courtesy to warn somebody before you jam a biomech socket into their back.

LAIONE: When will it be ready?

TROUT: Probably tonight. It needs time to settle in and heal before I can attach the rest. If your body rejects it, we'll need the extra time. No healing tanks, remember?

LAIONE: Right.

*(A pounding on the door)*

SHEENA: Mel? I need to talk to you.

*(*MEL *goes to the door.)*

MEL: Are you okay?

SHEENA: You lied to me, Mel.

MEL: What are you talking about?

SHEENA: I found where the birdbrain fell. Right where I thought, further north than you said.

MEL: Guess I remembered wrong. Like I said.

SHEENA: You're lying to me. I found the spot where it fell *and* the trail leading away from it. That trail leads here.

(SHEENA *pushes past* MEL *into the room. She sees* LAIONE. LAIONE *sees her. A tense instant, then* LAIONE *lunges.* MEL *grabs for them, but misses.* TROUT *watches.*)

(LAIONE *crashes into* SHEENA. *They struggle.* LAIONE *is stronger, even wounded.*)

MEL: Enough!

(MEL *grabs onto* LAIONE *and tries to pull them off.* LAIONE *ignores her.* SHEENA *finally manages to pull her rifle from her back and swings at* LAIONE. *The motion startles* LAIONE *into letting go, and* SHEENA *scrambles away.* TROUT *retrieves the gun from under the pallet in the corner.*)

MEL: Stop it, both of you!

(SHEENA *gets to her feet.* LAIONE *wraps their claws around her neck.* SHEENA *has her gun aimed at* LAIONE. TROUT *fires twice into the air; the gun lets out two enormous booms that resonate through the room. All freeze.*)

TROUT: That's enough of that, I think.

SHEENA: Not until this motherfucker's bleeding on the floor.

LAIONE: I'll enjoy tearing your throat out.

SHEENA: I took you down once, I can do it again.

LAIONE: You got lucky. You won't this time.

MEL: For Pete's sake.

(TROUT *hands her the gun.* MEL *holds it to the back of* LAIONE'*s head.*)

MEL: Hurt her, and I'll kill you myself. Sheena. Put the gun down.

SHEENA: Over my dead body.

LAIONE: Gladly.

MEL: You're both going to bring the Legion down on our heads.

LAIONE: It'd be worth it.

MEL: Do you want to fly again, or not? Sheena. The gun. Now.

SHEENA: Make your pet birdbrain let go of me first.

MEL: Trust me. I'll cover you.

SHEENA: The hell would I trust you when you've been hiding this from me?

TROUT: How about this? On three, all at once.

MEL: Fine by me.

*(Long pause)*

SHEENA: Fine.

*(Pause)*

LAIONE: Fine.

TROUT: Excellent. One, two, three.

*(On three, they split. SHEENA ends up near the door. LAIONE ends up in the opposite corner. MEL is between them. Something flickers past the window. No one notices.)*

LAIONE: If I see you again, I'll kill you.

SHEENA: You wanna go? Let's go.

MEL: That's enough.

SHEENA: Come on. You're so sure you can kill me, come outside and do it already.

*(LAIONE steps forward. MEL holds up a hand, and they reluctantly stop.)*

SHEENA: No? Gonna hide behind your little human friend, huh?

MEL: Sheena—

SHEENA: Fuck you, Mel. *(She leaves.)*

MEL: Damnit.

TROUT: Well. That was fun.

LAIONE: My gun.

*(The drone begins in the distance.)*

LAIONE: You threatened me.

MEL: I had to get Sheena to back down.

LAIONE: And if she hadn't? If I'd torn out her throat like my claws still itch to? Would you have fired?

MEL: To save her? Yes. You must have friends you'd do the same for.

LAIONE: My flock. Yes.

MEL: So.

LAIONE: I understand your reasoning. I want my gun back.
If I was going to kill you, I wouldn't need it.

MEL: I want your word you won't go after Sheena.

LAIONE: You'd trust the word of a birdbrain like me?

MEL: Yes.

LAIONE: And if I say no?

MEL: I guess we figure out which one of us is faster.

LAIONE: Loyalty. You'd make a good Legionnaire.

*(The drone is right overhead. Both humans eye the ceiling.)*

LAIONE: That's a supply ship. They can't hear you. You must know that.

TROUT: That gun of yours is loud. They could have.

MEL: It's not about them hearing us.

LAIONE: No?

MEL: It's about making sure they keep going.

*(A moment. The drone passes into the distance.)*

MEL: Your word.

LAIONE: You have it.

*(*MEL *hands the gun to* LAIONE.*)*

LAIONE: I make no promises if she comes after me.

MEL: Fair enough.

TROUT: We're rapidly approaching the point of no return here, Mel. I think it's time you explained how you're planning to pull this off.

MEL: Guess so.

*(*MEL *unearths a rusty lockbox from under the table or the piles of debris. She pulls her dog tag chain out from under her shirt and uses a small key on it to unlock the box. Inside is a small glass jar containing a strange substance.)*

TROUT: Chimeric.

MEL: I grabbed it when everything went to shit. That last day.

*(*TROUT *holds out a hand. After a moment,* MEL *carefully hands over the jar.)*

TROUT: They hunted down every single scientist involved in the program and had them killed. Looking for this, right?

LAIONE: Yes.

MEL: You made it out.

LAIONE: You worked with Chimeric? How did you survive the purge?

TROUT: Paranoia has its perks.

MEL: So does discretion.

LAIONE: That's not an answer.

TROUT: This is a good sample.

MEL: Certainly cost me enough to get it here.

TROUT: The Rebellion would kill for this.

LAIONE: The Legion, too.

TROUT: Why is that?

LAIONE: It's dangerous.

TROUT: Not really, in the grand scheme of things. And you haven't hunted down the Rebellion with nearly the vigor that you did the Chimera Project.

LAIONE: We were just told that it was dangerous. I don't know any more than that.

(TROUT *reluctantly hands the jar back.* MEL *replaces the jar in the box. The drone begins.*)

TROUT: Well. That does change things. I'll need a sample of your DNA, Laione.

LAIONE: For what?

TROUT: It's part of the Chimeric process.

LAIONE: You're not putting that stuff in me. Find another way.

TROUT: Don't worry. It's not for you, it's for Mel.

LAIONE: Fine.

TROUT: Excellent. I've got to make a run to my lab for supplies; Mel, I should be back before dark.

MEL: Stay safe. Lot of flyovers today.

(*The drone passes overhead and fades away.* TROUT *exits.* MEL *goes back to work.*)

LAIONE: What will you do?

MEL: Hm?

LAIONE: If you get your wings.

MEL: What will you do?

LAIONE: Go back to the Legion, of course.

MEL: Why?

LAIONE: My flock is there.

MEL: You said that before. Your 'flock'. What does that mean?

LAIONE: The others I fly with. We were recruited together. Trained together.

MEL: So they're your friends.

LAIONE: I suppose.

MEL: Do you miss them?

LAIONE: I'm concerned that they'll be punished for my disappearance.

MEL: But do you miss them?

LAIONE: What will you do, Mel?

*(Pause)*

MEL: Go.

LAIONE: Go where?

MEL: Somewhere free.

LAIONE: There is nowhere left. The Legion is everywhere.

MEL: Maybe. I intend to find out.

LAIONE: And your flock? Your friends. You'll leave them behind?

MEL: If I have to.

*(The door opens.* SHEENA *enters, a diminutive form slung over her shoulder.)*

SHEENA: Found this little rat sneaking around outside.

MEL: What—

SHEENA: Seeing as you're starting up a home for wayward aliens, figured it's your problem.

(SHEENA *tosses the form down and exits.* LAIONE *and* MEL
*look at the alien;* HAZE.)

MEL: Shit.

LAIONE: A TRACKER.

MEL: How long before more of you follow?

LAIONE: Depends when she was supposed to report
back.

(*A pause*)

MEL: You didn't signal—

LAIONE: No.

MEL: Don't suppose she'd spill her secrets to a friendly
face?

LAIONE: Not to a traitor.

(*Transition. Time passes. The radio crackles to life.*)

RADIO 4:
Now wailing in fear,
we rowed on up those
straits, Scylla to starboard,
dreaded Charybdis off to
port, her horrible
whirlpool gulping the
sea-surge down, down
but when she spewed it
up—like a cauldron over
a raging fire—all her
churning depths would
seethe and heave—
exploding spray
showering down to
splatter the peaks of both
crags at once!

(MEL *clears away any*
*machinery or delicate parts,*
*stashing them in various*
*crates and bins.* LAIONE
*hides their gun.*)


(MEL *pauses by the Chimeric,*
*hesitant.* LAIONE *sits on the*
*cot, watching.* MEL *looks at*
*them. Eye contact. A moment.*
MEL *puts the box away in the*
*same place as before and*
*departs. The door locks behind*
*her.*)

RADIO 7:
South Aurora reporting in.

This morning, Gecko took
a boat out into the Gulf.
We hoped that, with the
Legion focusing on
Omaha and whatever's
happening in the
Northwest, we'd have a
chance to slip the net.
He hasn't come back.
Maybe he got through
and made landfall in the
Caribbean somewhere.
Maybe the Legion sunk
him and he's on the
bottom of the ocean.
Only time will tell, I guess.

RADIO 8:
This is Hawk. Whatever's
happening around
Olympia is kicking off.
We've seen a two hundred
percent increase in Legion
activity in the area. All
western Ember squads,
lie low until whatever
this is passes over. It's
not worth getting killed
unless we have a real shot.

## Scene 4

(*Later.* LAIONE *sits in the same place.* HAZE *lies in a
crumpled heap by the stairs.*)

(LAIONE *waits, impatient. Taps their foot. Finally, gets up
and goes to* HAZE, *nudging her in the side with their foot.*)

LAIONE: Get up. Get *up*.

(HAZE *groans.*)

LAIONE: About time.

HAZE: My head…where is this? I saw a human.

LAIONE: Not soon enough, apparently.

HAZE: She snuck up on me.

LAIONE: A Legion tracker bested by one measly human? Embarrassing.

HAZE: What about you? I'm guessing you're Laione.

LAIONE: I am.

HAZE: You get shot down by one measly human? *(Pause)* Where are we?

LAIONE: What do you remember?

HAZE: Last place you called in was the top of the mountain, so I started there. I had your scent from your flock, so it only took me a few hours to find where you fell. Then I followed the smell east through the valley. I found this place ages ago, but I thought it was just a ruin. A pile of rotting wood and broken stone. I had no idea this was down here underneath all that mess. I thought maybe whatever was dragging you had gone through the river, lost the scent. But then I heard a noise, something loud, and circled back. I'd just gotten close when some human clubbed me over the back of the head.
What do *you* remember?

LAIONE: I was shot down. I crash landed on the mountainside. I woke up in this…pit, with a human crouched over me.

HAZE: You've been here this whole time?

LAIONE: Yes.

HAZE: And they haven't killed you?

LAIONE: They want something.

HAZE: Where are they now?

LAIONE: Gone to see if more were coming.

HAZE: How many?

LAIONE: Are more coming?

HAZE: Yes.

LAIONE: When?

HAZE: I don't know. A few days. I'm supposed to report in three.

*(A drone approaches. HAZE and LAIONE ignore it.)*

HAZE: What happened to your wings?

LAIONE: I lost one in the fall.

HAZE: What about the other?

LAIONE: Damaged.

*(The drone passes overhead and fades away.)*

HAZE: How long do we have?

LAIONE: Not long. They've been gone a while.

HAZE: Then we need to move quickly. *(She gets to her feet and tries the door. She prowls the room, studying the windows, the walls. Finds the radio.)* What's this?

LAIONE: Some kind of primitive communications receiver.

HAZE: How do you know that?

LAIONE: I've heard it. Voices. Music, sometimes.

HAZE: What do they say?

LAIONE: I've only heard bits and pieces.

*(HAZE touches a couple of dials. Fiddles. The radio crackles on. Static rises and falls. A distorted voice can be heard as HAZE turns the dials.)*

RADIO 4: All burst into applause, urging passage home for their parting guest, his farewell rang so true. Hallowed King Alcinous briskly called his herald: "Come, Pontonous! Mix the wine in the bowl, pour rounds to all our banqueters in the house, so we, with a prayer to mighty Zeus the Father, can sail our new friend home to native land."

HAZE: What is this? Some kind of code?

LAIONE: I have no idea.

HAZE: Can it send a message out?

LAIONE: I don't think so. I haven't seen them do so, anyway.

HAZE: What use is a one-way communications device?

*(LAIONE shrugs. HAZE turns the radio off and continues prowling the room.)*

HAZE: Well? Help me.

LAIONE: I've looked.

HAZE: Look again. We need to get out of here.

LAIONE: I've been here nearly a week. You're not going to find anything.

HAZE: I'm smaller than you. It's worth a look. What are they after?

LAIONE: Tech.

HAZE: How many are there?

LAIONE: Three that I've seen.

HAZE: Rebels?

LAIONE: I don't think so. They're on their own.

HAZE: If they're after tech, why are you—we—still alive?

LAIONE: Information.

HAZE: Ha. Good luck.

*(A drone approaches, crosses, fades. The dialogue continues unabated.)*

LAIONE: I've never heard of a tracker sent after one missing scout.

HAZE: The evidence pointed to humans.

LAIONE: So? There are plenty of humans still roaming the empty places of this world.

HAZE: They hijacked a supply ship. Grand Commander wants to make an example.

LAIONE: Right.

HAZE: Is something wrong?

LAIONE: Other than being grounded and at the mercy of a bunch of humans, you mean?

HAZE: Fair enough.

LAIONE: Part of me wants them to just end it already.

HAZE: Rather than be tortured for information?

LAIONE: No. Rather than face life on the ground.

*(Pause)*

HAZE: It's not so bad. You'll be fine.

*(A moment. A drone approaches, crosses, and fades.)*

LAIONE: One of the humans promised to replace my wing.

HAZE: They're lying. Why would they, when they have you locked up in here?

LAIONE: Why would they lie? Why say it at all if it isn't true.

HAZE: Who knows. Who cares? Humans are illogical, stubborn, chaotic creatures. Maybe they think it's funny.

LAIONE: Maybe.

HAZE: Besides. The Legion can do that.

LAIONE: The Legion could.

HAZE: In return for finding a few human escapees? The Legion *would*.

LAIONE: I can't take that chance.

HAZE: What?

(HAZE *turns to regard* LAIONE. *A moment. A realization*)

HAZE: Traitor.

(HAZE *lunges.* LAIONE *is stronger, and has more reach. They fend off* HAZE's *attack easily, until* HAZE *retreats, panting.*)

HAZE: How did they turn you?

LAIONE: I just told you.

HAZE: I should've known. Your kind have never been loyal. You're weak. Disobedient. What makes you think they won't just kill you when they have what they want?

LAIONE: What makes you think I won't just kill them? I haven't sold any secrets. I've not jeopardized the Legion.

HAZE: Liar.

LAIONE: One of them wants the same thing I do.

HAZE: And what's that? The death of the Legion? Their planet, returned to them so they can finish destroying it?

LAIONE: No.

HAZE: What, then?

LAIONE: Does it matter?

HAZE: Sure. It matters whether I tell Command that you were a traitor, or just crazy.

LAIONE: The sky. She promised to give me back the sky.

HAZE: And that's all it took? As if. Lying won't save you when the Legion comes.

LAIONE: When the Legion comes, I will be whole. I will hand them three human insurgents and a stockpile of Chimeric. That should be enough to buy my life.

*(A drone approaches, crosses, fades.)*

HAZE: The human has Chimeric?

LAIONE: Maybe the last of it, from what they've said.

HAZE: Call the Legion in. You have to.

LAIONE: No.

HAZE: Remember the code. Loyalty. Obedience. Strength. That's not just one way. They'll help you.

LAIONE: Will they?

HAZE: The Legion saved my people. That's what they do. They can save you, too.
Don't do this.

LAIONE: I have to.

HAZE: You don't. Trust the Legion.

LAIONE: I can't.

HAZE: Then help me escape. Tell the humans I got away.

LAIONE: They're human, not stupid. And you'll bring the Legion down too soon. Won't you?

HAZE: I could delay them. Give you a couple of days.

LAIONE: But you won't.

HAZE: The Chimeric will kill you. They don't
know how to use it. You've heard the stories. The
experiments. The things they found in the bunker.

LAIONE: Their scientist knows enough.

HAZE: The Legion knows more. The Legion could build
you a better wing than these humans can. Call them.
Let them help you.
Think of your people. Your flock. They'll be branded
traitors, too. Do you want that?

LAIONE: Of course not.

HAZE: They told me about you, you know. Your flock.
They said you were a model Scout. What happened to
you in this pit to change that?

LAIONE: There's a bomb.

HAZE: What?

LAIONE: The human has a bomb. If the Legion comes
here, they'll die. We all will.

HAZE: So disable it. Or take it away from here. Throw it
in the lake.

LAIONE: They'll know it was me.

HAZE: So what? You can take a few humans, right?

LAIONE: Of course I can.

HAZE: But you won't, will you? Disloyalty is in your
blood.

LAIONE: You know nothing about me.

HAZE: I know your kind. The Legion should've wiped
you all out when you rebelled. Made an example for
the rest of us.

LAIONE: That's enough.

*(Pause. A drone begins, crosses, fades. Two short raps on the
door. LAIONE produces their gun, and takes aim at HAZE.)*

LAIONE: Over there.

(LAIONE *nods to the closet from Scene 1.* HAZE *reluctantly complies.*)

HAZE: They'll kill me.

LAIONE: Not yet.

HAZE: And if you're wrong?

LAIONE: Not my problem.
I'll do what I can.

(LAIONE *whistles a signal. The door clicks and opens, and* MEL *and* TROUT *enter.*)

MEL: What did you find out?

LAIONE: Three days.

MEL: That's not much time.

HAZE: Give yourselves up. You can't outrun the Legion.

TROUT: Hush. Hold still.

(TROUT *approaches with a hypodermic needle.* HAZE *backs away.*)

HAZE: What is that?

MEL: A sedative. To keep you out of trouble.

HAZE: Get away from me!

LAIONE: I can always shoot you, if you'd prefer.

(HAZE *reluctantly allows* TROUT *to give her the shot.*)

LAIONE: Now. In there.

TROUT: You may want to sit down before that kicks in.

HAZE: You can't be serious.

MEL: Deadly.

LAIONE: Do it.

(HAZE *climbs into the closet and shuts the door.* MEL *crosses and locks it.*)

MEL: Three days isn't a lot of time.

TROUT: You're lucky I'm brilliant. *(Ze fishes the bio port out from zer pocket.)* It's ready for a test run.

*(The drone begins.)*

MEL: *(to* LAIONE*)* You ready?

LAIONE: Yes.

MEL: If this works, how long before you have mine ready?

TROUT: By morning, if you supply the coffee.

MEL: You got it.

*(The drone is right overhead. This time, it doesn't fade. It pulses in and out as the aircraft circles the area. The stage falls into a tense silence until, finally, it departs. All breathe.)*

MEL: Not good.

TROUT: No time to waste. *(To* LAIONE*)* Lie down on the table, please.

*(*LAIONE *does, carefully.* TROUT *begins prepping their back.)*

TROUT: I won't lie to you—this is going to do a bit more than sting. And I'll need you to keep perfectly still.

LAIONE: Fine.

TROUT: Mel will make sure of it, if you don't mind.

LAIONE: I'll be *fine.*

TROUT: You're sure?

LAIONE: Just do it, human.

*(*MEL *and* TROUT *make eye contact.* MEL *shrugs.* TROUT *shrugs.)*

TROUT: Alright. Here we go.

(TROUT *puts the port to* LAIONE's *wing stump. A buzzing noise.* LAIONE *groans.*)

MEL: Steady.

LAIONE: Shut up.

TROUT: Sixty seconds, starting now.

LAIONE: It burns.

TROUT: I know.

(LAIONE *tries to keep still, but the pain is growing.*)

MEL: Steady.

LAIONE: I know.

(*It is a long, tense minute. The buzzing builds. A muffled thud from inside the closet.*)

(*Finally, the buzzing abruptly cuts out and* LAIONE *collapses to the table.*)

TROUT: Well. It didn't reject outright. That's a good sign.

LAIONE: How long until we know for sure?

TROUT: Hopefully, by the time Mel finishes the wings.

LAIONE: That's reassuring.

TROUT: Sarcasm. Also a good sign.
Mel, you're up.

MEL: Right.

(MEL *strips off her shirt unceremoniously. Her torso is striped with scars. She turns her back to* TROUT, *who produces a syringe filled with Chimeric.*)

LAIONE: What…?

TROUT: My own little cocktail. A serum made from your DNA, mixed with a liberal dash of Chimeric.

LAIONE: What…does it do?

MEL: You don't know?

LAIONE: We were told it was dangerous, but never why.

TROUT: It rewrites DNA. Well, not rewrites it, exactly. Tweaks it. But it needs a blueprint.

MEL: And thanks to you, we have one.

TROUT: Ready?

MEL: Yes.

TROUT: Deep breath in.

(MEL *does.*)

TROUT: And out.

(MEL *does. As she breathes out, Trout slides the needle into her back and depresses the plunger until it is empty. By the end,* MEL's *breath is a hiss of pain.*)

MEL: Mother*fucker.*

TROUT: It will die down in a minute or two.

MEL: I remember. (*She braces herself on the table. The muscles of her back shift under her skin.*) Ah, shit.

TROUT: Breathe through it.

(*A drone passes overhead, lingers, and fades.* MEL *straightens, moving stiffly, and puts her shirt back on. She goes to the bin full of wing parts and begins to lay them out on the table.*)

TROUT: Better?

MEL: Bearable.

TROUT: I'll get to work on those other ports.

LAIONE: What can I do?

MEL: I could use an extra pair of hands.

LAIONE: You have them.

(*Transition. The sun sets; full dark outside the windows. The radio:*)

RADIO 3:
Warning to all Rebellion
operations in the Pacific
Northwest. If you're based
anywhere within a
hundred miles of
Olympia, evacuate
immediately. The Legion
is gearing up for
something big. I repeat:
warning to all Rebellion
operations in the Pacific
Northwest.

RADIO 9:
Testing. Testing. Is it
finally working? This is
Badger. You know, that
crazy asshole who stole a
Legion ship a few days
ago. We're still on the
ship. I repeat, we still
have the ship. The
Legion's been on our
asses, but so far we've
managed to avoid them.
Repeat, we are still flying
free. Keep your eyes on
the skies, my friends,
because we're not going
down without a fight.

RADIO 4:
I don't know if anyone is
listening. I hope you are.
If you are, I thought I'd
take a break tonight;
I have a little something

(TROUT *and* LAIONE *depart.*
MEL *is left alone onstage.*
*Her back is clearly misshapen,*
*distorting her shirt in strange*
*ways. She moves stiffly, but*
*never stops. She works. The*
*framework of a wing takes*
*shape on the table.)*

special this time around.
Hope you enjoy.

*(Music plays. Violin, or flute; something simple, lonely, and clearly played live.)*

## Scene 5

*(The middle of the night. MEL is alone onstage, working. Rolls of thick canvas lean against one side of the table. The frame of one wing leans against the wall, while a second is being constructed on the table. The music still plays from the radio.)*

*(The door opens. SHEENA enters, slowly. She stops just inside the door and folds her arms, watching for a long moment.)*

SHEENA: A note. That's all I get. A fucking note.

MEL: I didn't want to push.

SHEENA: What'd you do with the rat?

MEL: In the closet.

SHEENA: Dead?

MEL: Sedated. Trout says she'll be good until morning.

SHEENA: Lot of effort to keep that thing alive.

MEL: Might need her.

SHEENA: You're full of shit.

*(As MEL works, she shifts so the moonlight from the windows falls across her back.)*

SHEENA: Mel, what the hell have you done?

MEL: What I said I was going to.

SHEENA: Bet it hurts.

MEL: It does.

SHEENA: Good. *(Pause)* Well. You wanted to talk, so talk.

MEL: What do you want me to say?

SHEENA: Fuck that. Fuck you.

MEL: What?

SHEENA: If you don't have anything to say, then this is a waste of time. Do *you* want to talk or not?

MEL: I do. I just don't know where to start.

SHEENA: Sounds like that's your problem.

*(SHEENA starts to exit.)*

MEL: I'm sorry.

SHEENA: For?

MEL: Lying to you.

SHEENA: That's a start.

MEL: It was a chickenshit thing to do. I knew we were going to have this fight, I should've just come out and had it.

SHEENA: Yeah, you should have.
That it? Because I have a Legion invasion to prepare for.

MEL: I think…

SHEENA: What?

MEL: I think maybe you should go.

SHEENA: You asked me to come, Mel.

MEL: No, I mean—the Rebellion. I think you should go to the Rebellion. If you wait much longer, the Legion will be here and it'll be too late.

SHEENA: But you won't come with me.

MEL: I can't.

SHEENA: You can.

MEL: You're right. I won't.
This isn't your fight, Sheena. It never has been.

SHEENA: See, now that almost sounds like an apology.

MEL: It's not supposed to be.

SHEENA: Because you don't regret it, do you? Saving the bird.

MEL: No.

(Pause)

SHEENA: What the hell are you doing, Mel? Turning traitor?

MEL: I'm not a traitor. Who am I betraying?

SHEENA: Me, for starters.

MEL: This has nothing to do with you.

SHEENA: You're making deals with the Legion!

MEL: Not with the Legion. With Laione.

SHEENA: Same thing.

MEL: No.

SHEENA: What's the endgame here, Mel? You honestly think the Legion's going to let you go?

MEL: Maybe.

SHEENA: They'll chase you down. Maybe cut you up to see whatever you've done to your back.
What *have* you done?

MEL: Do you really need me to tell you?

SHEENA: Just give me a straight answer.

MEL: Okay. Chimera.

(Long pause)

SHEENA: You're kidding.

MEL: Nope.

SHEENA: You have—

MEL: Yep.

SHEENA: Why didn't you ever—

MEL: You would've wanted me to get rid of it.

SHEENA: No, I—

MEL: Or give it to the Rebellion.

(SHEENA *stops. A moment)*

MEL: I thought you didn't support the Chimera Project.

SHEENA: I didn't. I don't.

MEL: But.

SHEENA: Desperate times.

MEL: Desperate measures.
The Chimeric's useless to them, anyway. They'd need the catalyst.

SHEENA: You're saying you don't have some of that squirreled away, too?

MEL: No.

SHEENA: Then…?

(MEL *stops working.)*

MEL: The only catalyst I have is already inside me.
I was a part of the project. You must've figured that out by now. We were so close, everything was prepped, and then…

SHEENA: The Legion.

MEL: The fucking Legion. So I grabbed what I could and ran. I'm not surprised Trout ended up here, too.

SHEENA: Trout was—

MEL: As far as I know, ze's the only one left. Besides me.

SHEENA: Why would ze come here, then? Wouldn't it make more sense to split up?

MEL: Maybe. I think ze wants to complete the experiment. And I'm the only guinea pig left.

SHEENA: Mel… Every story I heard said the people who came out of that program weren't right. Were changed.
You don't know what that stuff's been doing to you. This whole crazy quest, sparing aliens left and right— it could all be because that shit is messing with your head.

MEL: I have dreams sometimes. Vivid…almost Technicolor. Like nothing else I've ever had.

SHEENA: Good or bad?

MEL: Some of both. But I usually don't want to wake up from them.

(Pause)

SHEENA: This is never going to work, Mel. There's too much that can go wrong.

MEL: Tell me about it.

SHEENA: That birdbrain's going to stab you in the back, first of all.

MEL: Maybe.

SHEENA: Oh, come on.

MEL: I'm not saying they won't. They might. I'm working on it.

SHEENA: And yet you're letting them run around willy nilly with Trout? The one person who's absolutely critical to this stupid scheme?

MEL: Laione wants to fly as much as I do. Maybe more. They won't jeopardize that until they have what they want.

SHEENA: And what then?

MEL: We'll see.

SHEENA: In the right hands, that stuff could turn the tide of the war.

MEL: What war? The war's been over for years.

SHEENA: No, it hasn't.

MEL: The Rebellion is just a dream, Sheena. That's all. I've seen the Legion in action, and those people don't stand a chance.

SHEENA: They would if people like you and Trout would help them.

MEL: It wouldn't make a difference.

SHEENA: How can you know that if you haven't even tried?

MEL: I don't believe in them, Sheena. In it. Nothing short of a goddamn miracle is gonna drive the Legion off now. I don't believe the Rebellion is it.

SHEENA: I do.

MEL: I know.

SHEENA: You say you don't believe. I don't believe you.

MEL: Why's that?

SHEENA: You still listen to the radio.

MEL: So?

SHEENA: Why would you listen if you didn't think something important was going to happen?

MEL: To bear witness. It's the end of the world, at least the one we knew. Least I can do is witness it.

SHEENA: Mel, we do have a chance. The Legion's been hunting Badger and her crew for a week and they haven't caught them yet.

MEL: Because Badger's crazy enough to get lucky. Doesn't mean anything.

SHEENA: We have a chance.

MEL: Look. I'm glad you still believe, Sheena. Someone has to. But you didn't see what I did. You were barely out of boot when we lost the war. Did you ever see New York? Or Chicago? Or San Francisco?

SHEENA: No.

MEL: What the Legion did to those cities… All the Rebellion's going to do is piss off the Legion enough that they get bombed into oblivion, too. Best case scenario, they don't take anyone else with them. Worst case, the Legion decides this entire planet is better off without us and finishes what they started.

SHEENA: You can't really believe that.

MEL: I really, really wish I didn't.

SHEENA: If the Legion's so big, bad, and scary, do you really think you can get away from them?

MEL: I think I have to try. I'm so tired of this, Sheena. One way or another, I want it to be over. Maybe this way, it can be a happy ending.

SHEENA: Mel…

MEL: I have to do this.

SHEENA: You're going to get us all killed.

MEL: Don't put that on me.

SHEENA: That's the choice you're making.

MEL: No one's making you stay.

(Pause)

SHEENA: That's how it's gonna be, huh?

MEL: Guess so.

(The door opens. LAIONE steps inside. A tense moment.)

MEL: Sheena was just leaving.

LAIONE: By all means.

(*They step aside. Another long moment.* SHEENA *exits.*)

MEL: How's your back?

LAIONE: Fine. Yours?

MEL: Hurts.

LAIONE: How long does it last?

MEL: A while. I'm used to it.

LAIONE: Chimeric?

MEL: Pain.

(LAIONE *crosses to look at the wing against the wall.*)

LAIONE: Yours or mine?

MEL: Mine. Wanted to start with a smaller one. This one's yours.

LAIONE: I would've thought you'd do both of yours first.

MEL: Your port will be ready sooner. Makes sense not to leave yours for last.

LAIONE: I mean.

MEL: Yeah. I know. (*Pause*) You're really going back, when all this is done?

LAIONE: Of course. What else could I do?

MEL: Anything. It's a big planet. You probably know better than I do where the holes are to slip through.

LAIONE: The Legion is all I know.

MEL: Is that a good enough reason to go back? Aren't you curious?

LAIONE: You humans and your curiosity.

MEL: I mean it. Don't get me wrong, the Pacific Northwest is gorgeous, but there's so much more out there.

LAIONE: Where would I go?

MEL: Anywhere you want.

LAIONE: Want.

MEL: What do you want?

LAIONE: No one's ever asked me that before.

MEL: Never?

LAIONE: Never.
It doesn't matter what I want. The Legion is where I belong.

MEL: Tell me about it.

LAIONE: About the Legion?

MEL: Yeah. The Legion you know. I can't understand why you'd want to go back, but I'd like to.

*(Long pause.)*

LAIONE: In the Legion, you know who you are, because you are who you're told to be. I'm a scout. I've always been a scout, and I always will be. It's—not easy—but simple, to do well. You don't have to ask yourself questions about whether or not it's the right thing to be doing, or if it's what you want, because you weren't given another option.

MEL: See, that sounds like hell to me.

LAIONE: And what would you rather have? Free will, so you can keep making a mess of things? The Legion saved you from yourselves.

MEL: So they say. But we were turning it around.

LAIONE: Really.

MEL: Really. We've always fought amongst ourselves.
We've always struggled, and backslid, and made
things worse. And then we've always picked ourselves
back up and kept trying. We've done horrible things
as a species, yeah. But we've done a lot of good things,
too. Whenever one person chooses to do a horrible
thing, ten more stand up and choose to try and do the
right thing.

LAIONE: And what is the right thing?

MEL: There's no easy answer to that. It's just…what
feels right at the time.

LAIONE: And sparing me? Is that what felt right?

MEL: I needed you alive for the Chimeric.

LAIONE: You didn't need me awake.

MEL: Yeah, it's what felt right.

LAIONE: Why?

MEL: I don't know about the rest of the world, but the
population of the US was four hundred million before.
Now, we've got what?

LAIONE: Maybe a quarter of that. Probably less.

MEL: It felt like there'd been enough killing.

LAIONE: Sheena would have taken her revenge out on
me. Why didn't you?

*(Pause)*

MEL: I was there. When you first landed.

LAIONE: What?

MEL: Before the war. Before the ultimatum. Before we
knew what you were going to do. I was there when
that first ship landed on the runway at Dulles. I bet
there's only a half dozen humans left alive who were
there that day, who've seen a Commander in person.
And you know what's funny? I don't remember what

it looked like. I have no idea. All I remember is the way the morning sunlight caught the wings of the Scouts in the honor guard. The way their feathers gleamed like spun gold. It was the most beautiful thing I've ever seen. Like you'd stepped out of my dreams and into reality. If I'd died on that runway, right then, I would've died happy.

But I didn't. Instead, I got back in my jet, and two days later I was shooting you out of the sky. The only feathers I saw were on the bodies after they hit the ground, stained black with blood. I hate the Legion for that. For what they've done to us, and for what they made me do. I don't think I'll ever forgive them. But I'm so tired of fighting, Wings. Maybe you'll stab me in the back still. I really don't know. But it felt like I had to try.

LAIONE: Try what?

MEL: Maybe we never had to be enemies. That's all.

LAIONE: You hate the Legion. You just said so yourself.

MEL: You are not the Legion. (*She winces, staggers, catches herself on the table.*)

LAIONE: Mel?

MEL: My back. (*She groans.*) Something's wrong.

LAIONE: What?

MEL: I don't—I don't know.

LAIONE: Trout. We need Trout.

(MEL *nods.*)

LAIONE: Okay. Come on.

(*Transition.* LAIONE *helps* MEL *out. The door clicks behind them.*)

(*The stage is empty for a long moment.*)

*(The closet door jiggles. A thud. A crack. It opens, and* HAZE's *head pokes out. She scans the room. Climbs out, crosses to the door, and tests it. It's locked. She circles.)*

*(The radio crackles. Distorted voices.* HAZE *eyes it. She looks at the bomb. She searches the room, locates* LAIONE's *belt. Removes a small device from it and activates it. It starts to emit a high, barely-audible whine.)*

*(*HAZE *takes the device, retreats to the closet, and closes it behind her.)*

## Scene 6

*(The next day.* MEL *works at the table, a little shaky, but upright. The ports have been installed in her back, but she's clearly in pain.)*

LAIONE: Shouldn't you rest?

MEL: No time. We're behind.

TROUT: That's one way to put it.

LAIONE: What happened? You said you knew what you were doing.

TROUT: I did. I do.
In theory.
We never got to finish the project. You interrupted us, remember?

MEL: It's fine. I knew the risks. And I'm fine.

TROUT: See? She's fine.
Let me see your back, Laione. One close call is enough for me.

*(*LAIONE *allows zer to check their back.)*

LAIONE: Is it ready?

TROUT: No sign of rejection, which is good. By the time your wing is ready tonight, your back should be as well.

LAIONE: Good.

TROUT: You might be a bit asymmetrical, but at least you'll be airborne.

LAIONE: I'll take it.

TROUT: *(With a nod to the closet)* About time for another dose.

MEL: Be my guest.

*(Thudding footsteps. SHEENA enters in a hurry.)*

LAIONE: You!

SHEENA: No time, birdbrain. Something's wrong!

MEL: What?

SHEENA: The Legion's coming.

MEL: What the hell? How?

SHEENA: There are Legion flyers overhead. Squads of them.

MEL: What?

SHEENA: They started out in the next valley over, but they've been zeroing in. They know.

TROUT: How?

SHEENA: Somehow they know where to look. Maybe *someone* tipped them off.

LAIONE: It wasn't me. If I'd wanted to signal the Legion, I'd have done it before now.
Wait. *(They find their belt in the pile and check it.)* My distress beacon. It's gone. *(They cross to the closet.)* What did you do?

HAZE: What you should've done a long time ago.

SHEENA: She signaled them.

HAZE: They're coming. You can't stop it, now.

MEL: A day. We needed one. More. Goddamn. Day.

LAIONE: They're too close. They'll find us.

(LAIONE *pulls* HAZE *from the closet.*)

LAIONE: You stupid, loyalist *rat*. What harm would one more day have done?

(HAZE *grins.* SHEENA *shoves past them, finds the distress beacon in the closet, and destroys it.*)

SHEENA: There. That should slow them down. We need to go. Now!

MEL: We're so *close.*

SHEENA: Breaking it might have stalled them a bit, but they'll find this place before nightfall. We need to *go,* Mel! Set your bomb and let's get out of here!

TROUT: *(Raising zer voice)* We will NOT.

*(All stop and stare at* TROUT.*)*

TROUT: I have not come this far to let this experiment fail now.

SHEENA: Trout, they're coming. We can't stop them.

*(A pause)*

LAIONE: A diversion. Draw their attention somewhere else.

MEL: The radio tower.

SHEENA: No.

MEL: Sheena, it's the only way. It'll draw their attention, / give us the time that we need—

SHEENA: The only way is to *run.* We can go to the Rebellion, they'll hide us—

MEL: I am not running.

SHEENA: Mel, think about what you're doing/ for five goddamn seconds—

MEL: I <u>have</u> thought about it. Every damn day my whole life I've thought about it, dreamed about it, wished for it, as long as I can remember it's been the last thing I think about at night and sometimes it's the first thing I think about when I wake up because it's the only thing I dream about anymore. I've chased this my whole damn life. Keeping birds on the farm, reading books about falconry, lying on my back in the fields after the harvest and watching them soaring way overhead and wishing that I could follow them, and I tried; I joined the Navy, worked my ass off for my pilot's license, but without the wind on my face, what was the damn point? I signed up for some seriously sketchy experiments where they shot god knows what into my body and just when I thought I might finally do it, aliens take over the world. What are the fucking odds? So I grabbed what I could and ran and somehow, miraculously, against all odds, *finally* I might be able to do it, and you want me to drop it and run to the Rebellion. I've got nothing to give them, Sheena. I'm tired. The farm's burnt, everyone's dead, the Legion's boot is slowly, brutally crushing our collective necks, and this is the *only* thing that keeps me going anymore. Don't ask me to give it up. I can't. I'll chase this crazy, stupid dream all the way to hell if I have to. If you don't want to come with me, that's fine. I get that. But stop pinning my feet to the ground when I might finally be able to leave it.

*(Stunned silence)*

MEL: Please.

SHEENA: It's that important to you?

MEL: It's all I have.

SHEENA: Okay. I can't make you leave.

MEL: Thank you.

SHEENA: What can I do?

MEL: Take the bomb to the radio tower. I'll prime it, so all you have to do is press a button and run.

SHEENA: What if it doesn't work? What if the Legion comes here anyway and your contingency's wasted?

MEL: I guess I'll go down swinging.

SHEENA: No. If I do this and it doesn't buy us enough time, if the Legion comes, you come with me. We go to the Rebellion—

MEL: Sheena—

SHEENA: And I'll make sure they give you the time and space you need to finish this. But you're not dying here, Mel. Not if I can help it.

MEL: Okay. Deal.

SHEENA: Give me the damn bomb.

(MEL *grabs it, fiddles.*)

MEL: There. Set for ten minutes. Timer starts when you press this button.

SHEENA: Idiot proof.

MEL: Be careful.

SHEENA: Work fast. (*She exits.*)

MEL: How much time did that buy us?

LAIONE: Maybe twelve hours. A day, at absolute most.

MEL: That's not enough *time.*

LAIONE: Your back.

TROUT: I may have a solution.

HAZE: It doesn't matter how long you stall. They'll find you. I'll find you. I've been smelling your stink for days, and I never lose a scent.

MEL: Okay. Well. *(She holds out a hand to* LAIONE.*)* May I borrow your gun?

TROUT: Mine is quieter.

*(*TROUT *produces a small pistol and hands it to* MEL. *She takes aim at* HAZE.*)*

HAZE: I thought you said there'd been enough killing.

MEL: Listening in, were you?

HAZE: How could I not?

MEL: You're not leaving me much of a choice. *(She removes the safety.)*

HAZE: Wait. I can—if you spare me, I can convince the Legion not to kill you.

MEL: Really.

LAIONE: Unlikely.

HAZE: I can. I promise.

MEL: Maybe. But I don't want to live under Legion rule. That's the whole point.

HAZE: You don't have a choice. It's that or die here.

MEL: Yeah.

*(*MEL *fires.* HAZE *slumps to the floor. A long moment of stillness.* MEL *hands the gun back to* TROUT.*)*

MEL: We have work to do.

TROUT: Right. As I was saying, I have a stash of that healing spray the Legion brought that I've been trying to pick apart. I might be convinced to part with some of it.

MEL: In return for?

TROUT: The rest of your Chimeric. And a blood sample. Maybe I can rebuild the catalyst.

MEL: Done.

TROUT: I'll even throw in a little body disposal.

MEL: Fine.

TROUT: Right. I'll be back, then.

MEL: Watch yourself.

(TROUT *scoops up* HAZE's *body and exits.* MEL *looks at the blood on the ground for a long moment.*)

MEL: Why are they doing this?

LAIONE: What do you mean?

MEL: Three humans in the middle of nowhere. We're no threat. We're barely surviving as it is. Why do they even care?

LAIONE: Because they learned the hard way not to give any quarter.

MEL: That sounds like a story.

LAIONE: My people were named for the clouds, once. The closest translation you have is 'Cirrus'. We had a hundred different names for the wind. And then the Legion came, and wanted to turn us into nothing more than Scouts. Some of us didn't agree. Some of us fought.

MEL: And?

LAIONE: We lost, of course.

MEL: Of course.

LAIONE: We became Scouts. Most of us forgot what we used to be. Some didn't just forget; they were afraid to remember.

MEL: How long ago was that?

LAIONE: Centuries. Before my time. But some Cirrus remember, and they pass it down. I never paid any attention. I figured it was just looking for trouble.

MEL: Or looking for hope.

LAIONE: Is there a difference? We rebelled once, you know. Thousands of us were killed for it, and in the end, nothing changed. The Legion is too strong to fight.

MEL: Fighting isn't the only way to rebel.
Cirrus is a beautiful name.

*(LAIONE looks at the blood on the ground.)*

MEL: Help me finish this.

*(Transition. MEL and LAIONE work. The radio crackles to life, staticky, subdued.)*

RADIO 5:
Axolotl here, from Scranton. We just got back from New York this morning. I don't…I don't even know where to start. There wasn't a single building left standing in any of the five boroughs. The ground was…like swiss cheese. More hole than solid ground. We set down in Manhattan. Maybe because all the bridges were out, so they knew we couldn't run. Not a lot of bodies on the street. I don't know if they've rotted away or the Legion cleaned them up. I didn't ask. But we had to cut through the subway, once, because 5th Avenue was blocked by debris. The subway tunnels are just graves

*(TROUT returns. They put the finishing touches on all three wings.)*

*(An explosion rocks the stage. The windows go red. The radio tower burns in the distance. The radio fizzles out into static.)*

*(SHEENA returns, a small pack of belongings in tow. She watches them work. The wings are attached, one by one; LAIONE's while they lie on the cot. MEL's while she lies on the table.)*

now. People piled against
the walls. I don't know
what killed them. I don't
know if I want to.

RADIO 4:
You in your day have
witnessed funeral games
for many heroes, games
to honor the death of
kings, when young men
cinch their belts, tense
to win some prize— but
if you'd laid eyes on
these it would have
thrilled your heart,
magnificent trophies
the goddess, glistening-
footed Thetis, held out
in your honor. You were
dear to the gods, so even
in death your name will
never die… Great glory
is yours, Achilles, for all
time, in the eyes of all
mankind! But I? What
joy for me when the coil
of war had wound down?

RADIO 1:
At approximately 0200
hours last night, the
Legion ship flown by
Badger was spotted
coming south over the
Great Lakes, with several
fighter ships in hot pursuit.
At 0215, the ship went

down into the waters of
Lake Superior. We've kept
watch on the shores. So far,
there do not appear to be
any survivors. This is,
however, Badger we're
talking about. We will
continue to watch.

## Scene 7

*(Predawn.* LAIONE *and* MEL *doze fitfully.* SHEENA *fiddles with the radio.* TROUT *packs a small bag, including the case with the Chimeric inside. Ze heads for the door.)*

SHEENA: You're leaving?

TROUT: Yes?

SHEENA: Now?

TROUT: The proverbial shit is about to hit the proverbial fan, my dear. Has already, really; we're just waiting to see who gets hit with the worst of it as it comes down. I intend to be under cover, myself.

SHEENA: Where?

TROUT: I have my hidey holes. When things die down in a few days, I'll move along, just to be safe.

SHEENA: You could come with me to the Rebellion. They could use your smarts.

TROUT: Join your doomed little army? I don't think so.

SHEENA: My doomed little—?

TROUT: That came out a bit harsher than I'd meant it to. But I suppose it's true.

SHEENA: The Rebellion has a chance.

TROUT: If that's what you need to sleep at night.
For what it's worth, I wish you good luck. I wish I
could hang around to see if the wings work, but I'd
rather make it through this day alive. *(Ze exits.)*

MEL: Sheena…

SHEENA: You're awake.

MEL: Never really got to sleep.
Listen. There's a car. I stashed it on the other side of the
mountain, at the end of the access road. It might run a
little rusty, but it's solar powered. Should give you a
head start.

SHEENA: You said you would come with me.

MEL: If we didn't finish. We did.

SHEENA: You don't even know if they work.

MEL: Only one way to find out. I'm either flying or
dying here, Sheena. And either way, I'm not going
to the Rebellion. But you should. They need you.
Especially now that Badger's gone.

SHEENA: She's not gone. This is Badger we're talking
about.

MEL: Exactly. They need somebody else who won't
give up.

SHEENA: What do I have that they need? I'm a decent
marksman, sure, but apart from that?

MEL: You believe.

SHEENA: What?

MEL: You still believe we can win this fight. I'm
guessing that's something they're running real short on
over there.
Take the car. Go fight your fight. I hope you win.

SHEENA: You should be coming with me.

MEL: Maybe one day I will. Who knows?

SHEENA: Here. Take this. *(She rummages in her pack and retrieves a small handheld radio.)*

MEL: Sheena—

SHEENA: Just in case. I'll use the one in your car. And this way, you'll know… if it's ever safe to come home. Small enough to fly with and everything.

MEL: Okay.

*(SHEENA hands the radio to MEL.)*

SHEENA: God. If you make it… I hope you make it. I hope it's everything you want it to be.

MEL: You, too.

*(Slowly, painfully, MEL sits up. The wings drape awkwardly behind her.)*

MEL: Good luck, Sheena.

SHEENA: Good luck, Mel.

*(SHEENA picks up her belongings and exits.)*

*(LAIONE stirs. They sit up, slowly, wincing. They stand. Carefully, they flex their wings: one tattered, organic; the other, sleek and metallic. Matching, and yet completely different. They runs a hand across the new wing.)*

*(The drone begins to fade in. Deeper, bigger than it has been before. LAIONE's hand falls to their gun. MEL raises her head. They look at each other.)*

MEL: I need a decision, Laione.

LAIONE: You'll never outrun them.

MEL: Never know unless I try.

LAIONE: Turning you in could buy me a promotion. Forgiveness for everything that happened here.

MEL: It could. *(A long pause)* It's a big world.

LAIONE: I think… I'd like to see it.

(LAIONE *take their hand off the gun.* MEL *smiles.*)

MEL: Then come with me.

(MEL *pockets the radio. A pounding on the door. Voices shouting indistinctly.* MEL *and* LAIONE *exchange a look.*)

(*A shot rings out, then another. Panicked shouting. The sound of people running, shots firing.*)

MEL: Sheena. She was supposed to—damn it!

(MEL *runs to the window. A shape flashes past. Some of the voices fade as they give chase.*)

MEL: *Now* she runs.

LAIONE: She's giving us cover. Don't waste it. Are you ready?

MEL: Absolutely.

(*Together,* MEL *and* LAIONE *open their wings. They are massive, spanning the stage, tattered and imperfect and beautiful. Blackout. Cacophony. The sound of wings.*)

### END OF PLAY

# RADIO VOICES

*There are nine distinct voices on the radio in this play. My recommendation is to pre-record the radio voices, rather than having actors from the main cast speak from offstage. It is important to have as many different voices on the radio as possible, to help the world of the Legion feel fully populated.*

*Each voice is listed with any identifying information and when it appears in the script. If identity is not specified, feel free to cast however you choose. Each voice should be consistent across all appearances.*

RADIO 1—*Rebellion member, part of the Web. An observer. Based in the Midwest. Appears in Scenes 1 and 6.*

RADIO 2—*Raven. Trans man, Rebellion informant based in the Norman, Oklahoma Legion settlement. Appears in Scene 1.*

RADIO 3—*Rebellion member, part of the Web. An observer. Based in Nevada. Appears in Scenes 1 and 4.*

RADIO 4—*Civilian. Could be anyone. Appears in Scenes 1, 2, 3, 4 (Mid and end), and 6.*

RADIO 5—*Axolotl. Rebellion informant based in the Scranton, Pennsylvania Legion settlement. Appears in Scenes 2 and 6.*

RADIO 6—*Croc, southern Rebel leader. Woman, Southern accent preferred. Appears in Scene 2.*

RADIO 7—*Rebellion member, non-combatant. Based somewhere in the southern US. Appears in Scene 3.*

RADIO 8—*Hawk, western Rebel leader. Woman, middle-aged or older. Appears in Scene 3.*

RADIO 9—*Badger, eastern Rebel leader. Woman, brash. Appears in Scene 4.*

# GLOSSARY OF LEGION CYCLE TERMS

**Aurora**—the noncombatant arm of the Rebellion. Responsible for supply runs, scientific work on captured Legion tech, etc.

**Badger**—Rebellion leader in the eastern US. If the Rebellion has a figurehead, it's her.

**(the) Chimera Project**—a last-ditch fringe effort by the US military to genetically alter soldiers to enable to them to fight the Legion more effectively.

**Chimeric**—a key aspect of the Chimera Project. Pronounced "KAI-mer-ic".

**Command**—the alien species that leads the Legion. Not much is known about them.

**Croc**—Rebellion leader in the southern US.

**Ember**—the combat arm of the Rebellion. Led by Badger, Hawk, and Croc.

**Hawk**—Rebellion leader in the western US. Cautious.

**Legionnaire's Code**—Loyalty, Obedience, Strength. The unifying rule by which the Legion operates.

**(the) Rebellion**—the human resistance to the Legion's occupation. Consists of three main branches, operating out of many decentralized cells. Rebellion members use animal monikers to hide their identities.

**Scout**—Avian aliens that work in flocks. Responsible for scouting new terrain and patrolling controlled terrain. Humans often refer to them derogatorily as "birdbrains".

**Tracker**—Ratlike aliens that generally work alone. Responsible for tracking down runaways.

**(the) Web**—the observation arm of the Rebellion. Web members watch and report, but generally do not actively participate in Rebellion actions.